# How the Good Times Rolled

### RICHARD FIDLER

## MISSION POINT PRESS

Readers are encouraged to go to www.Mission-PointPress.com to contact the author or to find information on how to buy this book in bulk at a discounted rate.

Published by Mission Point Press
2554 Chandler Rd.
Traverse City, MI 49686
(231) 421-9513
www.MissionPointPress.com

ISBN: 978-1-943995-71-4
Library of Congress Control Number: 2018941622

Printed in the United States of America.

## Illustration Acknowledgements

Benzie Area Historical Society
Pages 2; 6; 13; 70a

Leelanau Historical Society
Special recognition goes to the Jill Cheney collection.
Frontispiece; 4; 7; 29 (above); 35; 36; 40; 48; 52; 62; 98

Traverse Area District Library Local History Collection
All illustrations are from the Traverse City Area Historical Society collection unless noted otherwise. Special acknowledgement goes to the Liz Bannister Collection of Sheet Music.
iv; 2; 5; 8; 9 (Floyd Webster Photograph Collection); 10; 12; 14; 15; 16; 17; 18-19; 20; 22; 23; 24; 26; 28; 30; 32-33; 34; 37; 38; 39; 41; 42-43; 44; 45; 46; 53; 54; 55; 56; 57; 58; 59; 64; 66; 67; 68; 69; 72 (Bannister); 74 (Bannister); 75 (Bannister); 78; 80; 81; 82; 83; 85 (Bannister); 86; 88; 89; 90-91; 93; 94; 100; 102; 103; 104; 105; 108; 109; 110

Individuals
Richard Fidler: 60-61; 65
Julie Schopieray: 109
Heather Shaw: vii; 25

# CONTENTS

# BEFORE, WHAT DID WE DO FOR FUN?

Every day I go out and observe what people are doing. I see them walking on the sidewalk, driving the car, eating in restaurants, working out at the gym, and hanging out with their friends. I read the newspaper — yes, I still do that — and I look at what is offered for entertainment. I keep up on the news by way of the internet, too, exploring a variety of sites every day. As much as any other person, I am aware of what is going on, though I might not be as connected to the worlds of the young and of those racially separated from the mainstream of society as I could be.

What I see is a people preoccupied with communication. They watch human interactions on television, they visit websites, they participate in Facebook and Twitter, they do email, they constantly talk with friends and those they barely know with their iPhones, they watch movies on Netflix, they play video games. When they go to the gym, they interact with their phones as they are exercising. I have seen individuals walking their dogs in the woods while texting to a friend. In the bookstore where I go for coffee every morning, the patrons sit alone staring at their communication device while sipping coffee and eating a sweet roll. Young and old, wealthy or near poor, male or female — everyone is talking to each other.

Circus elephants parade along Traverse City's Front Street, 1890's.

Clear on what we *are* doing, I formed the question, "What are we *not* doing (that we used to) as we pass the hours of our lives? I thought I already knew, but — as is the custom nowadays — I would need to check my preconceptions by visiting the internet. And so I did: in rapid succession, I placed phrases into the search engine: decline of reading; decline of attendance in cultural events; decline of hunting;

decline of fishing; decline of dancing. In every case, paydirt: a plethora of articles supporting my preconceptions. We no longer do those things that used to be so important to us.

Approaching the question from another angle, I began to read old newspapers from Traverse City, Michigan, those from a hundred or more years ago. What did they tell us about how people spent their time back then? I was especially interested in how they spent their leisure time, not the time they put in working or taking care of the family or going to church. How did they enjoy themselves?

Beyond the newspapers, I have access to a fine collection of historic photographs, the Traverse Area Historical Society collection maintained by the Traverse Area District Library, and began to pay attention to what sort of images were preserved for later generations. In addition, the photograph collections of the Leelanau Museum and Historical Society and the Benzie Museum and Historical Society widened my experience with more stunning pictures. Folders of photographs of sports, hunting and fishing, celebrations, and organizations of every kind contained a visual record of times past, many showing staid portraits of individuals long passed, but others full of lively fun and good humor. Archives are windows into our history, windows through which we could begin to understand what we have lost as we stumble into this Brave New World of technology.

A hundred years ago, people connected directly, face-to-face with each other when they attended plays and movies, participated in clubs, and enjoyed individual and team sports, danced together, and met to play cards or play billiards. At the same time, they experienced plenty of alone time as they walked to work, went hunting and fishing, or read books on a quiet evening. Social interactions were not intrusive, as they came to be as telephone use spread. Instead, they were done by choice and often required effort, whether a visit to someone's house, attendance at a theater, or writing a postcard to a friend. Maintaining friendships and nurturing communities required work.

Those of us whose lives have encompassed some of this change — I am 74 years old — feel angst at seeing both the decline of face-to-face human interactions as well as the decline of time spent strictly alone. In providing accessibility to communication anywhere and anytime, technology has taken something from us, something that used to be very precious: our ability to sit quietly and simply talk. The irony may be that, as we find it easier to talk to others, we find ourselves less capable of achieving real communication. Are three-hour conversations with friends a thing of the past? Are we incapable of taking a walk in the woods, only paying attention to the wild things around us?

The kinds of photographs of people portrayed here are naturally limited by the nature of the collection from which they were taken. The archives I examined included views of the Traverse area dating from 1869 to the present. The community is, and always has been, primarily white, although a Native American presence has always existed. Traverse City has been a relatively small town for most of its existence, its population reaching 10,000 early in the twentieth century and growing slowly after that, not reaching 20,000 at the publication date of this book. Located towards the northern end of the Lower Peninsula of Michigan, it has been isolated from the currents of immigration that swept across the United States during the nineteenth and early twentieth centuries. To some extent, that may explain the lack of diversity in the area.

Still, the Traverse region does mirror the social milieu of America generally. It was swept up in the cultural changes of the twenties and beyond. Some photographs shown here will describe those changes, though many will remind us of things we generally associate with ages past — hunting and fishing, horse racing and county fairs. In 1900, 38 percent of Americans were farmers, a figure comparable to that of Grand Traverse County at that time. The photo record not only shows bucolic activities—like hunting — as well as urban ones — like a Shakespeare Club, but also shows glimmerings of the same cultural assets preserved in a big city like Detroit. I believe it is quite representative of American life at the time.

How were photographs selected for inclusion in this book? First, they had to correspond to leisure activities identified in newspaper articles and other documents between 1890 and the 1930's. Second, they had to meet basic standards of photographic excellence. That is not to say that old, tattered photos were rejected for artistic reasons; sometimes the content of the picture overrides all such considerations. Third, photographs of women's activities were included whenever possible. Since men are often shown more often than women in old picture collections, gender bias is hard to avoid. Here, at least, an effort has been made. Fourth, since a few images could not be obtained readily from the local collection, it was necessary to look elsewhere. Unable to find a suitable picture of roller skaters, for example, I chose to include a postcard showing them.

*Let the Good Times Roll* is mostly meant to be read for fun. It is, indeed, fun to look at a caravan of elephants walking down an unpaved Front Street or to view an old postcard that has the postcard maker embracing a skeleton, but at the same time, we should keep in mind the deeper reason this book was conceived: the need to confront the current separation of people from each other and the natural world. Something has been lost — we know it even if we are unable to articulate it. I hope that this volume will stimulate readers to reflect on their lives so that they might feel more connected to their communities. Using mirrors of the past, we can rebuild what we have lost.

Richard Fidler
May, 2018

Photo, facing page: Winton C. Hull and company in front of the Hannah-Lay building, Traverse City, ca. 1910

# OUTDOOR SPORTS

Swimming was popular years ago as well as now on public and private beaches. With more relaxed standards for female dress, women began to participate more and more, beginning in the twenties. At that time and before, cities and townships often built water slides and diving platforms — before they became discouraged by lawsuits focused on the possibility of accidents on such equipment.

The beach beckoned to all at resorts throughout the region. Before the age of auto tourism, families would stay much of the summer at a single resort, the father often staying at his job in the southern big cities. That meant time at the beach was a regular part of each day, not only for swimming but for rock collecting, sun bathing, and casually reading books and talking with friends. It was truly a vacation for all, never a frantic effort to see as many attractions as possible within an allotted time of a week or two.

Facing page: Frontenac Resort Sand Party, Frankfort, 1890's.
* * *
This page: Water slide at the Wequetong Club, Traverse City.

Launch carrying a party on Lake Leelanau, ca. 1900.

Speed Boat Race
at Traverse City, Mich.

Boating was popular, too, both at the resorts and privately on individual lakes. Boats came in all configurations, motorized launches that could accommodate ten or twenty resorters on excursions, sailboats for recreation or racing, motorboats for those inclined to speed, and rowboats for fishing or a leisurely tour of the lake shore. Boating was another reason to come to northern Michigan to enjoy summer.

Crystal Lake Yacht Club Sea Scow Sailing Race.

Boating Northport Point, Mich.

**B**icycles became popular in the United States in the 1890's with the creation of the "safety bicycle," a vehicle with chain and sprocket, wheels about the same size, a frame similar to that used today, and pneumatic tires. Its popularity soared as prices came down, though a bicycle could cost as much as 100 dollars in 1891, that sum equal to a fifth of a working man's salary at the time. By 1900, however, Sears and Roebuck mail order catalogue listed the item at 7.50, a price within range of most workers.

Men and women took to them for a variety of reasons. They gave riders the freedom to go where they wanted, no matter what the schedule of crowded trolleys. They were silent. They were fast. They offered good exercise. And they produced no manure!

Facing page: Two women with their bicycles, early 20th century.

* * *

This page: Woman on bicycle near Boardman Lake, Traverse City.

With such recommendations, by 1895 the bicycle club League of American Wheelmen had a million members. The fad lasted until the attractions of the automobile — after 1915 — overshadowed it. In response to traffic and pollution concerns, bicycling has made a comeback in recent years, with miles of paved paths providing safe riding routes for riders.

This page: A bicycle race held at the Driving Park (present Civic Center), Traverse City.

* * *

Facing page, clockwise from top left: *Detroit Free Press*, 1880; high-wheeler bicycle from the late 1800's; *Lansing State Journal*, 1915.

## "BICYCLE RIDERS MUST KEEP OFF WALKS," COLE

Bicycle riders must keep off the sidewalks this year, declared Chief of Police Cole, Monday morning. Last year three children were injured by riders on walks and Cole says he will prosecute violators vigorously this year. Herbert Jonson, 1500 West Allegan st., was the first violator to be arrested. He paid a $4 fine assessed by Justice Haight, Monday morning.

Tennis at Camp Arbutus

The first game of lawn tennis in the United States was recorded in 1874. By 1881 the first United States Championships were inaugurated, players (men, only) sporting blazers and cravats, knickerbockers, woolen stockings, and rubber-soled shoes. In the early twentieth century women were still bound by Puritan tradition, wearing long dresses. By the thirties,, short skirts and even shorts were boldly worn by women players, the great woman player Suzanne Lenglen leading the way.

Girls playing tennis, Camp Arbutus, Grand Traverse County about 1930.

Though tennis never became the favorite sport of Americans, it represented a happy confluence of athletics, fashion, and sexuality as expressed by its professional champions, both men and women. A game that started out as lobs over a net became a tense competition between players that gloried in a slam to the opposing court.

With the spread of hard court tennis after 1900, the game rapidly spread to country clubs, colleges, and high schools.

The days of grass courts were only a memory, except in the case of Wimbledon, of course.

*G*olf arrived late in the 19th century to the United States. Chicago, an early center of the game, boasted the first course in the Midwest, but its first players were not native-born Americans — most with Scottish roots.

The number of courses increased rapidly over following decades as people began to pay attention of the accomplishments of two American golfers, the amateur Bobby Jones and the professional, Walter Hagen. Both men dominated the game during the twenties and thirties.

Golf was one sport that did not reject the participation of women. The great Babe Didrikson Zaharias loved the game, inspiring many women to take it up. She won the US Women's Open in 1946, and continued her tournament successes into the early 1950's.

Man playing golf, Traverse City Country Club, ca. 1935.

PECK PHOTO

Postcard showing the Traverse City Country Club, ca. 1920.

Shuffleboard began as a shipboard game, but quickly became popular on land after 1913. As its popularity spread, Traverse City was the center of an important tournament. Above, Shuffleboard tournament, Traverse City, 1918.

Harness racing, Traverse City Driving Park (present Civic Center). Early 20th century.

\* \* \*

Following page: Traverse City Driving Park, early 20th century.

Horse racing was nearly always featured in country fairs throughout the country. In Michigan and other Midwestern communities, harness racing occurred in those venues, the horse pulling a two-wheeled carriage called a sulky with a pacing or trotting gait. Betting on horse races was a common practice, whether permitted by law or not. Harness racing reached its zenith at the beginning of the twentieth century, declined for a time, then regained some of its early popularity by 1980.

[ 17

20]

**TRAVERSE CITY DAY**

**Friday, July 22, 1910**

### Monster Picnic Dinner

Tables set for 5,000, Coffee and Sugar provided. 12:00 Noon, Standard Time.

### Cadillac-Traverse City League Ball game

Everything Free, Grand Stand, Bleachers; not one cent to pay. 3:00 p. m.

### Band Concert

and music all day long, commencing 10:00 a. m.

### Games and Sports

of all kinds for young and old, suitable prizes, no entrance fee. 10:30 a. m. 12:00 Noon.

### Good Speaking and Singing

Talks by Prominent Business Men and others. Good Music, Vocal Solos following immediately after dinner.

THIS IS YOUR INVITATION, and we are looking for you and and all your folks to be there. This is an invitation to every Farmer and Farmer's Family in Grand Traverse Region to be welcome guests of Traverse City and her hustling business men. WE HAVE ATTENDED TO THE GOOD TIME.

### All You Have to do is Come

Baseball became popular among both players and fans during the nineteenth and early twentieth centuries. It was played at all levels, amateur, high school, college, semi-professional, and professional from the inception of the National League in 1881 to the present day. The minor leagues, not always connected with major league teams, underwent cycles of popularity over the course of the twentieth century with at least 32 cities represented in eight leagues throughout the state of Michigan. However, by the thirties, the heart had gone out of minor league baseball. Teams would struggle to survive two or three seasons.

"Barnstormers" would frequently visit far-flung towns in Michigan to compete with local teams. Black teams from larger cities came to northern Michigan to play them, this encounter supplying cross-cultural experiences to people far removed from places of more diverse populations. One all-Indian team, the Bay Shore Indians, toured the state in 1910.

Admission to minor league games was approximately twenty-five cents, a bargain until you consider that a loaf of bread could be purchased for ten cents at that time. The working class could not afford to attend games on a regular basis, not only for its cost, but also because workers had to work six days a week. No doubt some still came when they could—to enjoy a pleasant day with the game, popcorn or peanuts, and the companionship of their friends.

Facing page: "A League Player," image from the 1890's.

\* \* \*

Left: Advertisement for the all-city picnic. (Described on page 109.)

Facing page: Rare photograph of a local women's baseball team, 1890's.

* * *

This page: Traverse City Baseball Club, photographed at the Driving Park (present Civic Center), 1911.

Fishing in all its forms — ice fishing, bait fishing in summer, fly fishing, fishing with nets, spearing — was carried on by Native Americans as well as white settlers. As white settlement disrupted habitats through dams and overfishing, certain species were drastically reduced (Lake sturgeon) or disappeared altogether (Arctic grayling). The Adams fly, invented by Len Halliday in 1922, put the tiny village of Kingsley, Michigan, on the map, at least in the experience of fly fishers the world over. A monument exists in the adjacent village of Mayfield to honor his achievement.

Facing page: Fly fisher cleaning catch, 1920's. Note the size of catch.

\* \* \*

This page: Young fisherman, Yuba, 1940s.

This page: Fishing camp, 1890's.

\* \* \*

Facing page: Beer barrel hijinks at fish camp.

The following description of ice fishing by Native Americans in 1859 is taken from the *Grand Traverse Herald*:

> The Indians are now engaged in fishing for them [Lake trout]. They cut a hole in the ice, cover it with evergreen boughs, throw in an artificial decoy fish attached to a line, throw themselves flat upon their faces, and, with spear in hand, watch the approach of the unsuspecting trout to the decoy, when, quick as lightning, the spear is thrust, and a ten or twenty pound trout is floundering on the ice.

The extreme sizes given for fish taken at this time may not have been exaggerations. Before 1850 when commercial fishing began in earnest on the Great Lakes, reported sizes of fish were much larger than those reported today.

Facing page: Fishermen, mid-20th century.

\* \* \*

This page, top: Ice Shanty, North Lake Leelanau, date unknown.

Bottom: Ice shanty, mid-Michigan, 1940s

This page: Hunting party, 1890's.

* * *

Facing page: Skeet shooting at the Wequetong Club, Traverse City.

*N*ot everyone owned guns a hundred or more years ago. City dwellers often did without, though farmers often had them, both to get rid of pests as well as for hunting. Considering that 38 percent of Americans lived on farms in 1900, it is fair to say that firearm ownership was common at this time.

Skeet shooting was practiced in the early years of the twentieth century and displays of marksmanship impressed audiences all over the United States. Buffalo Bill's Wild West Show featured the great Annie Oakley who became a legend for her skills with a variety of guns.

Young people often used firearms, often in ways that would trouble us now. In some towns, anti-rat, anti-crow, anti-sparrow campaigns were carried on by young people who would bring in small bodies (or parts of them) in order to receive rewards from local officials. Presumably the missed shots did not bother those who had to put up with broken windows and occasional injury.

Hunting was very popular with those living close in the country. Predators like bear and wolves were hunted and killed for trophies and because they were regarded as nuisances. Deer hunting provided venison to households, the meat often contributing significantly to the family's nutrition. Birds were hunted, too, for that purpose, grouse, ducks, geese, and passenger pigeons supplying the targets. The last passenger pigeon was killed about the turn of the twentieth century, a victim of an age in which there were no limits to the number of animals killed.

Hunters, 1890's.

Couple in early auto, 1913.

Dune buggy, Leelanau folder: Autos were used as thrill rides on
Sleeping Bear dunes.  Photo from the 1960's.

he auto meant liberation for early drivers. Liberation from the necessity of keeping horses. Liberation from the dirty, tightly scheduled railroads as auto-touring began. Liberation for women drivers, who were suddenly free to leave the home to shop and visit friends. Liberation in dating as the man could pick up his lady and take her somewhere far from her parents' critical eyes.

The introduction of the Model T Ford in 1908 made car ownership possible for the middle class who had been priced out of the market before that time. By 1929 sixty percent of American households owned an automobile, the total number of vehicles increasing steadily after that, reaching a peak in 2010.

An early "snowmobile," Leland.

Couple kissing in automobile, 1913.

Cars were modern, sexy, and especially attractive to the young. The chorus to the popular 1905 song In My Merry Oldsmobile speaks to the joy of the motorcar. The double entendre at the end is, no doubt, intended:

> Come away with me, Lucille
> In my merry Oldsmobile
> Down the road of life we'll fly
> Automobubbling, you and I
>
> To the church we'll swiftly steal
> Then our wedding bells will peal
> You can go as far as you like with me
> In my merry Oldsmobile.

This page: Mule-drawn sleigh.

\* \* \*

Facing page: Toboggan run located on the Country Club grounds,
Traverse City, 1920's.

For most of the United States, skiing belonged to certain ethnic groups — the Finns and Scandinavians above all — and was seldom practiced in the late-nineteenth and early-twentieth centuries. Instead, those in search of thrills in a snowy environment sought out toboggans, sleds without runners that could accommodate many riders at one time.

The 1880's saw a blossoming of the toboggan fad. Many communities set up toboggan slides towering up to sixty feet high, the chute packed with frozen slush. Riders could coast for a quarter of a mile or more after the descent.

Fashion designers responded to the public's passion for tobogganing with toboggan suits for women, clothing better adapted to snow play than the long dresses in fashion at the time.

The building of tall slides ended abruptly by the 1890's, perhaps due to the death of a celebrity in a toboggan accident. The sport had a short-lived resurgence in the twenties, but generally declined after that, sports lovers preferring skis and ski boards to toboggans.

SKATING ON BOARDMAN LAKE, TRAVERSE CITY, MICH.

Facing page: Toboggan ride, Leelanau County.

# INDOOR SPORTS

*F*ew sports have such a well-defined beginning as basketball. James Naismith, the inventor of the game, published his thirteen rules for the game in the Triangle, a newsletter distributed to all the YMCAs of the world. Immediately teams sprang up, in YMCAs, colleges, and small town gyms everywhere. Basketball invaded high schools, too, even providing sport for young women—who were obliged to play in bloomers, that costume often deemed so risqué in the Victorian era that men were not allowed to watch. The rules of the women's basketball took note of the "weaker constitutions of the fair sex" by limiting the size of the court and by promoting a less intense physical style. Besides women, other groups took up the game. For example, by the 1920's touring teams of black basketball players joined in the fun. Across America, basketball became enormously popular with both genders, all ethnic and racial groups, and with people of all ages.

Previous page: Girls high school basketball team, ca. 1900.
* * *
This page: Boys basketball game, 1940's.

DALE. PARK.

TRAVERSE CITY. MICH.

The *Traverse City Evening Record* informed its readers about a wrestling (and boxing) contest held in 1908. According to the account, the losing wrestler was unable to make his crotch and wrist hold stick, that failure accounting for his loss. The paper goes on to say:

As the wrestling match is the first professional match that has been carried off in this city for about 10 years, it was not expected that the interest manifested by those who were present is indicative of the character of the performance. The sporting blood of Traverse City received a quickening, and it is probably that this is the beginning of a revival of similar affairs.

…A number of ladies in the audience last night watched the performance with interest, and had it been more generally known that ladies would be present, there would have been many more in attendance. There was nothing in the affair to offend the most refined tastes, and the few ladies who attended evinced as much pleasure as their gentlemen friends.

## MT. CLEMENS OBJECTS TO ROLLER SKATERS

**Health Seekers Claim They Are Menace to Life and Limb, and Want Protection.**

Mt. Clemens, Mich., June 7.—A complaint will be laid before the city council at their next meeting by residents on Mullet street relative to children using the sidewalks of that street for roller skating. Several cripples who come to the city for the baths have had narrow escapes from being injured by skaters running into them. The board has had the matter up before this, but no action has been taken. The residents of the street will demand

This page, left: Roller skating dancers Julie Bradford and Harold Telgard, Traverse City.

Above: *Detroit Free Press*, 1913.

\* \* \*

Facing page, top: Two roller skate performers, about 1940.

Bottom: *Detroit Free Press*, 1908.

## ROLLER SKATING ON AVENUES BECOMES DETROIT SOCIETY FAD

Asphalt Pavements in Aristocratic Sections of the City Scenes
of Merry Parties and Parlors Are
Transformed Into Rinks.

Roller skating, though invented many years before, became popular in the 1880's in the United States. The sport declined and rose in popularity over the course of the next 120 years. Indoor roller skating rinks appeared early on, and provided a place where young men and women could meet and enjoy each other's company.

Some evenings a band would play as skaters danced to the melodies, as this account from the Traverse City Evening Record describes:

> For three hours last evening 200 people shod on skates with slippery rollers fitted fore and aft, slewed, slipped, fell, tumbled and rolled upon the white solid flooring of the new auditorium to the time of a grand march played by a twelve-piece band stationed in the corner far out of harm's way. A general feeling of good will pervaded the atmosphere and if a sprawler insisted on sprawling, friendly hands placed him on his feet or gathered him together and sat him gently down on seats provided. Sometimes the greater energy was expended in attempting to do nothing, or in other words, it more often took a grater amount of energy to stand still than it did to go some. As long as motion was kept up, direction didn't count.
> — *Traverse City Evening Record*, March 23, 1906

[ 47

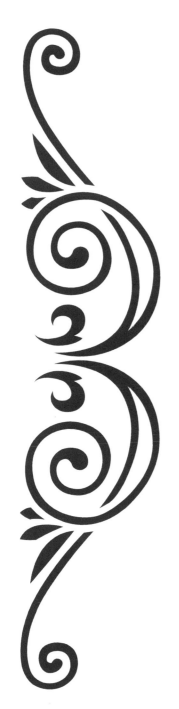

# SEDENTARY AMUSEMENTS

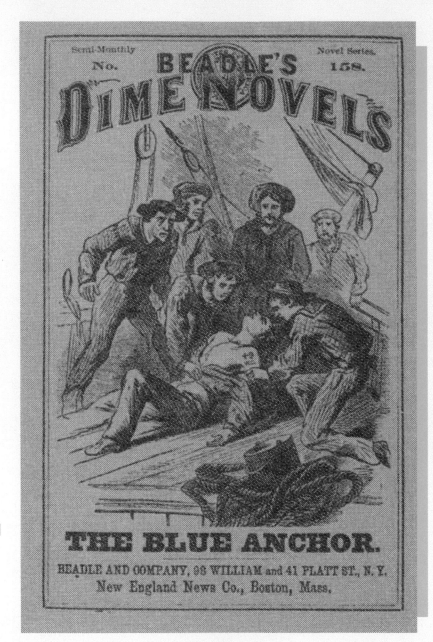

Previous page: domestic scene, turn of the twentieth century Attribute to Leelanau.

\* \* \*

Covers of typical dime novels. Note the "semi-monthly" statement.

People enjoyed reading at the turn of the twentieth century, but what did they read? The simple answer is that they read the same sort of books people do now, light fiction overwhelming all other categories for children and adults. According to figures obtained for the Traverse City Public Library in 1905, nonfiction categories took up scarcely a tenth of the number of novels circulated.

Between 1860 and 1910 the "dime novel," a short work of fiction totally about 100 pages in length, explored topics often forbidden in regular literature; sex, violence, racism, homosexuality, and gender issues were often addressed in that tight format. Dime novels were written by a committee usually consisting of several women who would identify stories that could be expanded into a novel, a person who orchestrated its production, a group of writers who sketched out the plot, and the actual author who completed the manuscript. From start to finish, the process might take a matter of weeks from conception to finished product. Such books were read across all social classes, but especially by the poor and near poor.

Western themes were common in dime novels.

Facing page: Reading at the Leelanau cottage, ca. 1900.

\* \* \*

This page: The Carnegie public library of Traverse City, Michigan.

Serialized novels were carried in many newspapers and magazines during the same period. Like dime novels, they were seen as a form of literature especially enjoyed by the lower class, especially after 1900. By 1940, they had largely disappeared.

Philanthropist Andrew Carnegie supported public libraries with generous grants for constructing new buildings in practically every town and city across the United States. At first, monthly counts were kept of those entering reading rooms for study or pleasure. Traverse City once counted 206 men, 77 women, and 773 children , figures that point to the library as a gathering place for the young. Amid the silence enforced in the reading room, did young boys and girls communicate nonverbally or with written notes passed among them? You can be sure they did.

a hundred years ago, postcards filled the niche now occupied by phone and texting. In 1913 more than 900 million were circulated in the United States, more than eight per citizen. They were informal, unlike regular letters, and allowed the sender to express greetings, consolation, seasonal cheer, or, on occasion, love. Comments were open for all to see — even the postman.

Since in large cities mail was delivered two or even three times a day, cryptic messages could be sent in the morning about a rendezvous in park and received in the afternoon. Communication was not as backward as we imagine now.

Postcards were cheap, only three to five cents a card. Postage in the early years of the twentieth century was set by law at one cent. Even by the standards of the day, they were inexpensive and fun, both to write and to receive. Until 1907 those sending postcards could not write on the backs. After that date, the split-back card enabled longer messages that did not mar the front.

IN INDIAN GARDEN

54]

MOONLIGHT FROM UNION STREET BRIDGE. TRAVERSE CITY, MICH.

Colored postcards appeared before World War I, most of coloring done in Germany. With the coming of that war, the quality of colored cards sank considerably, though the American postcard industry was quick to catch up to earlier high standards.

Postcard makers were found in every town and city. Some cards were no more than positives made from negatives that were the exact size of a postcard. Often in black-and-white, the first ones came out in 1901 with a Kodak camera designed for that purpose.

Facing page, top: Indian pavilion, Leelanau County, first decade of the 20th century.

Bottom: Postcard maker Orson W. Peck with skeleton.

\* \* \*

This page, top: Central Methodist church at night, Traverse City.

Bottom: A postcard showing a railroad snowplow in Leelanau County.

 56]

This page: Knights of Pithea conventioneers at play, ca. 1912.

* * *

Facing page: The Republican Club before the passage of Women's Suffrage.

At the peak of their popularity, it is estimated that as much as 40 percent of the adult population of the United States belonged to one or more of them. Most were segregated by gender and ethnicity. Black fraternal societies existed in some parts of the country, and women's lodges were formed as affiliates to men's parent organizations, such as the Rebekahs, a group affiliated with the Independent Order of Odd Fellows.

Fraternal Societies performed many functions within communities. They offered medical benefits for the sick, insurance for those in need, and retirement homes for the elderly. Ritual and mystery provided a platform that attracted the interest of many, while religious underpinnings, both Protestant and Catholic, united believers in accomplishing social goals such as food pantries and disaster relief.

During the thirties, social programs begun by Franklin Delano Roosevelt began to slow enrollment in fraternal societies. At the present time they still exert an influence on American society, but much less than in former times.

F raternal organizations like the Freemasons and the Odd Fellows grew in membership over the last third of the 19th and first part of the twentieth century. At the close of the Civil War, many new organizations were formed, including the Knights of Pythias, the Grange, and the Elks. Later in the 19th century, the Knights of Columbus, the Moose, and the Woodmen of the World made their appearance, each one distinguished by particular religious and philosophical characteristics..

March 15 1912

58 ]

Shakespeare Club, Traverse City.

Meeting of the Traverse City Ladies Library Association featuring marshmallows.

Jigsaw puzzles, invented in the 18th century, became popular at the end of the 19th as cardboard gradually came to replace wood. The first puzzles had few pieces and were used mostly to help children learn the states, for example. Later, as they came more complex, they came to be a source of recreation, one enjoyed by the whole family. Even during the Great Depression, when people had little money to spend, they were a popular form of home entertainment.

Early board games in the nineteenth century were about attaining religious peace and salvation as tokens moved along a defined path towards that goal. By the 1880's, the emphasis changed to obtaining material wealth and success. The beginnings of the game Monopoly (not called by that name) trace to 1904. Besides entertainment, the purpose of that game was educational: it showed that, over time, property came to be held by fewer and fewer people.

Checkers (called draughts in England) and chess, games with a long history, were popularly played throughout America.

Various card games were popular in the nineteenth century and before. Rummy, hearts, pinochle and euchre were all played at the end of the nineteenth century. Contract bridge dates from 1922.

Above: A jigsaw puzzle dated 1934. It was one of a monthly series sent out through the postal service. Price, twenty-five cents.

* * *

Facing page: The above jigsaw, put together.

WASHINGTON'S INAUGURATION AT PHILADELPHIA—1793

© THE FOUNDATION PRESS, INC.
CLEVELAND, OHIO

(No Model.)

E. J. BOND.
TOY OR GAME.

No. 446,054.                    Patented Feb. 10, 1891.

Fig. 1.

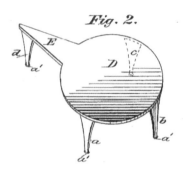

Fig. 2.

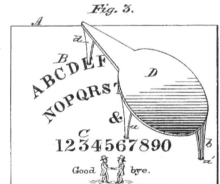

Fig. 3.

Witnesses:
Frank de Benzhyr
H. R. Walton,

Inventor:
Elijah J. Bond,
By T. C. Breckt,

Attorney.

# THE SATURDAY EVENING POST

Fou          nkly        nklin

MAY 1, 1920                    5c. THE COPY

Facing page: Leelanau card players: Date unknown.

* * *

This page, left: Elijah Bond's patent for the Ouija Board (US Patents).

Top: Norman Rockwell cover art showing a couple with Ouiji board.

Above: Party with card players, Traverse City, 1890's.

* * *

Facing page: Home pinball game, popular in the 1920's and 30's.

## LINDSTROM'S
### HY-BALL PIN GAME
### INSTRUCTIONS

Each player shoots seven marbles, one at a time.
The scoring value of each disc is plainly shown by the numerals appearing on the game. However when a marble enters a disc that has the same color as the marble, then the score is doubled.

For instance: the pink marble in the pink disc [300] scores double or 600. The red marble in the red disc [200] scores double or 400. When a marble of a different color enters a disc the score value is the same as appears on the game.

If one of the marbles is shot into the HORSESHOE then the entire score is doubled. For example: if the total score is 1200 and one of the marbles enters the HORSESHOE then the total score is doubled and becomes 2400.

M'f'g by
**Lindstrom Tool & Toy Co.**
**Bridgeport, Conn.**

Pinball was a game with a long history, the form that featured a spring launcher of marbles dating from 1971 in the United States. Primitive boards without electricity were played well into the twentieth century and coin-operated, electric displays appeared in the thirties.

66]

Gloria Swanson
in "Her Gilded Cage"
A PARAMOUNT PICTURE

Beginning in the 1890's and extending to the late 1920's, silent movies were immensely popular with audiences across the United States. For some films, sound could be provided by an organist with special sound effects within reach — the barking of dogs, the sound of a train whistle, or the roar of thunder. With technological improvements creating "talkies", the silent movie industry had ended by the 1930's, but not before dozens of stars had whetted America's appetite for film — Charlie Chaplain, Gloria Swanson, Rudolf Valentino, Buster Keaton, and Lilian Gish, to name only a few.

Show offerings would change on a weekly basis with some held over for longer runs. The price of a ticket — 25 cents — made it possible for workers sometimes making less than two dollars a day to watch a movie on an occasional basis.

Facing page: A flyer for a silent movie production.

A photo of the Lyric Theatre in Traverse City. Built in 1915, it was destroyed by fire in 1923, rebuilt, only to burn again in 1948. This picture is from the 30's.

JOSEPH M. SCHENCK
PRESENTS

# NORMA TALMADGE
IN
## "A DAUGHTER OF TWO WORLDS"
ADAPTED FROM THE FAMOUS NOVEL
BY LEROY SCOTT
DIRECTED BY JAMES YOUNG

68 ]

This page: Flyer for silent movie productions, early 1920's.

\* \* \*

Facing page: The ornate lobby of the Lyric Theatre, Traverse City.

"Who forged that check?" demanded Black Jerry, and the little daughter of the slums knew she must go to jail. ◆ ◆

JENNIE, the daughter of Black Jerry Malone, keeper of a low dance hall in the slums of New York, having associated with crooks all her life, is induced to forge checks and finally caught. Facing a prison sentence she is rescued, and after a time in a finishing school, is introduced into exclusive society. Her advent into the second of the two worlds results in a series of amazing adventures. A story of thrilling and absorbing interest, pictured by the fascinating

## NORMA TALMADGE
in "A DAUGHTER OF TWO WORLDS"

# LYRIC THEATRE
Tuesday and Wednesday
## APRIL 20th AND 21st

A "First National" Attraction

# MUSIC & DANCE

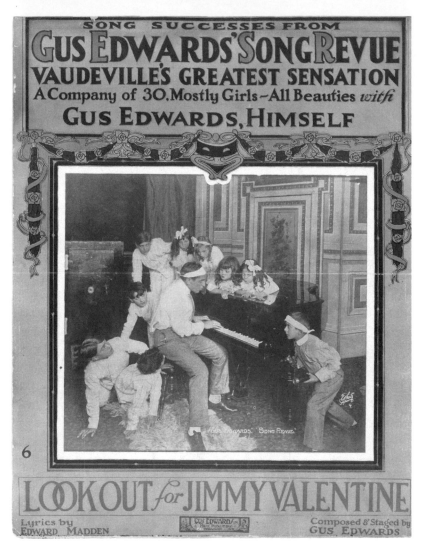

Miss May Vaughn, Singing Commedienne now at Dreamland.

A box containing a large python from India, an anaconda from South America, diamond back rattlers, water moccasins and copper heads, a collection of America's most vicious and poisonous snakes was received yesterday from San Antonio, Texas by Winn Gardner of 130 East Eighth Street. Mr. Gardner will work all of the snakes for an audience at Dreamland. He will take only one snake out of the box at a time so there will be no danger of any of them escaping and putting the spectators to flight.

72]

Previous page: Girls dancing at Camp Osoha-of-the-Dunes 1920's on Crystal Lake.

* * *

Right, top: "Miss May Vaughn, Singing Commedienne now at Dreamland."

Right text: News item from the *Traverse City Evening Record*, April 30, 1918.

Beginning in the 1880's, vaudeville brought entertainment to large and small venues across the United States. Jugglers, magicians, musicians, dancers, acrobats, actors, and especially comedians put on a variety of acts, often as many as twelve an evening, the performances often lasting for hours. They traveled the vaudeville circuit, the highest levels of which offered substantial pay for performers in an era before movies and radio.

Vaudeville, though still mired in racist attitudes in the early twentieth century, brought a variety of cross-cultural experiences to American audiences. Immigrants performed acts they had perfected in their homelands, and black dancers and singers commonly did song-and-dance routines in places far removed from black neighborhoods. With trained animal acts (sometimes developed abroad) and clownish routines, the show frequently took on a circus air.

By the 1930's vaudeville was on the way out, ticket sales dwindling in the face of competition from movie theaters. Some acts, like those of George and Gracie Burns and Bob Hope, were able to transition successfully into the new world of film (and later, TV), but most succumbed to the failing economics of the industry.

"Mr. and Mrs. Lew Stanley, Fashionable Singing Duo, now at Dreamland."

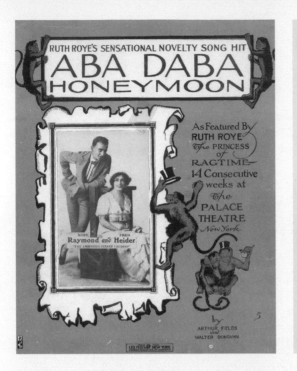

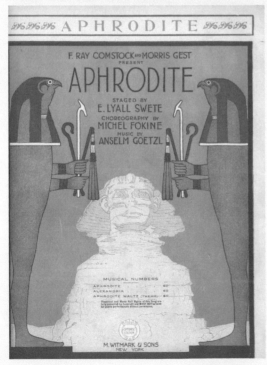

From the 1890's Tin Pan Alley in New York City was the center of the sheet music industry. It supplied music for vaudeville, bands, vocal groups, and for home entertainment. If householders could afford a piano, they frequently gathered around it to sing popular hits, old favorites, and musical celebrations of holidays. By 1930, phonograph records outsold sheet music as people began to perform music less and listen to it more.

76]

This page: Two advertisements for radio, 1938.

\* \* \*

Facing page: Radio schedule for Sunday, January 26, 1952.

# Radio Program

## TONIGHT
### ——(E.S.T)——

| NBC | MBS | CBS | ABC |
|---|---|---|---|
| 6:00 News | News | Record Parade | American Farmer |
| 6:15 Music of Yesterday | Dinner Music | Record Parade | American Farmer |
| 6:30 NBC Symphony | Sammy Kaye Time | Record Parade | Local |
| 6:45 NBC Symphony | Business Reporter | News | Local |
| 7:00 NBC Symphony | Sports Digest | Visiting Time | Local |
| 7:15 NBC Symphony | Twin Views of News | Visiting Time | Local |
| 7:30 Hello Sucker | Comedy of Errors | Operation Underground | Adam's Playroom |
| 7:45 Hello Sucker | 7:55 Cecil Brown | Operation Underground | Adam's Playroom |
| 8:00 Jane Ace | Twenty Questions | Gene Autry | Local |
| 8:15 Jane Ace | Twenty Questions | Gene Autry | Local |
| 8:30 Bob and Ray | Hockey Game | Hopalong Cassidy | Local |
| 8:45 Bob and Ray | Hockey Game | Hopalong Cassidy | Local |
| 9:00 Judy Canova Show | Hockey Game | Gangbusters | Dancing Party |
| 9:15 Judy Canova Show | Hockey Game | Gangbusters | Dancing Party |
| 9:30 Grand Ole Opry | Hockey Game | Broadway is My Beat | Great Adventure |
| 9:45 Grand Ole Opry | Hockey Game | Broadway is My Beat | Great Adventure |
| 10:00 Vaughn Monroe | Hockey Game | News | Chance of a Lifetime |
| 10:15 Show | Hockey Game | March of Dimes | Chance of a Lifetime |
| 10:30 Goodman Album | Variety Program | Frank York | Chance of a Lifetime |
| 10:45 Goodman Album | Variety Program | Frank York | Chance of a Lifetime |

## SUNDAY AFTERNOON AND EVENING

| NBC | MBS | CBS | ABC |
|---|---|---|---|
| 4:00 The Falcon | Glee Club | News | Revival Hour |
| 4:15 The Falcon | Glee Club | News, E. C. Hill | Revival Hour |
| 4:30 Martin Kane | Under Arrest | People's Platform | Revival Hour |
| 4:45 Martin Kane | Bobby Benson | People's Platform | Revival Hour |
| 5:00 Scotland Yard | The Shadow | Arthur's Round Table | Light and Life |
| 5:15 Scotland Yard | The Shadow | Arthur's Round Table | Light and Life |
| 5:30 The Silent Man | True Detective Mys. | Hearthstone of the | Greatest Story |
| 5:45 The Silent Man | True Detective Mys. | Death Squad | Greatest Story |
| 6:00 Texas Rangers | Gabby Hayes Show | My Friend Irma | Drew Pearson |
| 6:15 Texas Rangers | Gabby Hayes Show | My Friend Irma | Monday Morn. Headlines |
| 6:30 The Big Show | Nick Carter | Our Miss Brooks | Hour of Decision |
| 6:45 The Big Show | 6:55 Cecil Brown News | Our Miss Brooks | Hour of Decision |
| 7:00 The Big Show | Peter Salem | Jack Benny | National Vespers |
| 7:15 The Big Show | Peter Salem | Jack Benny | National Vespers |
| 7:30 The Big Show | Vesper Service | Amos 'n Andy | Fine Arts Quartet |
| 7:45 The Big Show | Vesper Service | Amos 'n Andy | Fine Arts Quartet |
| 8:00 Harris-Faye Show | Your Government | Charlie McCarthy | Stop the Music |
| 8:15 Harris-Faye Show | Your Government | Charlie McCarthy | Stop the Music |
| 8:30 Theater Guild | Enchanted Hour | Philip Morris Playhouse | Stop the Music |
| 8:45 Theater Guild | Enchanted Hour | Philip Morris Playhouse | Stop the Music |
| 9:00 Theater Guild | Opera Concert | Corliss Archer | Walter Winchell |
| 9:15 Theater Guild | Opera Concert | Corliss Archer | Cafe Istanbul |
| 9:30 To Be Announced | John J. Anthony Hour | Meet Millie | Cafe Istanbul |
| 4:45 To Be Announced | John J. Anthony Hour | Meet Millie | Three Suns |
| 10:00 S64 Question | Variety Program | News | Paul Harvey |
| 10:15 S64 Question | Variety Program | The People Act | Memos for Men |
| 10:30 Tin Pan Valley | Sign Off | Choraliers | The Red Head |
| 10:45 Tin Pan Valley | | Choraliers | The Red Head |

At first radio was conceived as a means to communicate with select audiences — ship-to-to-shore, for example, a use termed "narrowcasting" for it narrow focus. By the twenties, entrepreneurs understood its capability as a force for mass entertainment, establishing the first broadcasting networks, NBC and CBS. Early radio offered a balance of entertainment possibilities: comedy, drama, news, music, and sports. Vaudeville and Hollywood talent were recruited to star in radio productions: Bob Hope, Groucho Marx, Amos and Andy, Jack Benny, and Ronald Coleman, to name only a few.

Families would regularly sit down beside the radio, hope for good reception, and enjoy family shows together on Sundays and other special days, their listening interrupted with few commercials. With the advent of television in the 1950's, radio drama largely ended, standard formats emphasizing talk, music, news, and sports taking its place.

While Thomas Alva Edison's first phonograph appeared in 1878, the invention was slow to capture the interest of the US market. His invention, the phonograph, played wax cylinders, and required an electric motor and cumbersome batteries. By the 1890's he and his competitors came up with more practical crank models that sold for less than 10 dollars, an affordable price for the average American family.

Because these machines could play a recording for only two minutes, the kinds of music offered to the public were quite limited. Classical arias, band marches, and popular tunes constituted the bulk of the musical repertoire. Longer concert pieces would have to wait until technology improved enough to allow longer, better-quality recordings.

Disk playing machines — at first called gramophones—became popular in the first decade of the twentieth century, eventually driving the cylinder-playing competition out of business. By the 1920's almost all records were recorded by Victor Records or Columbia.

Some musical celebrities worried about the effects of the new technology on the American musical soul. John Philip Sousa wrote, "Under these conditions, the tide of amateurism cannot but recede until there will be left only the mechanical device and the professional executant. Singing will no longer be a fine accomplishment; vocal exercises will be out of vogue! Then what of the national throat? Will it not weaken? What of the national chest? Will it not shrink?"

His fears were not unfounded

Facing page: Beach party with gramophone, ca. 1913.

This page: Campbell's band, 1890.

* * *

Facing page: Men with folk instruments, ca. 1890.

*L*ocal groups of musicians performed for fun and money, their specialties ranging from orchestral music to folk tunes and popular songs. Music teachers made a (meager) living teaching specific musical instruments, though many musicians were self-taught. Frequent dancing parties and roller skating events required music of one sort or another: Friday and Saturday nights were lively places to be in Traverse City and other small towns.

americans sought out classical music years ago. Large cities had their own symphony orchestras, but smaller resort communities had their own concert venues. In Petoskey, Michigan, the Bay View Association brought classical music to its summer programs beginning in 1879. The Interlochen Arts Camp, founded in 1926, not only trained young musicians, but also featured performances by world-renowned composers and musical assemblages. Early radio further brought opera and symphonic music into homes during the 1920's, 30's, and beyond.

This page: Post card of a performance at the Interlochen National Music Camp Bowl.

* * *

Facing page: View from the stage of the Interlochen National Music Camp Bowl.

*a*mericans loved to dance from Revolutionary War days. Although some churches disapproved of it, balls, parties, and fund-raising events regularly attracted dancers at all skill levels. At first, older dances like waltzes and quadrilles were popular, but, by the 1890's, they were increasingly being replaced by the one-step and by "animal dances," such as the Lame Duck or the Grizzly Bear. Those dances, comical to us today, attempted to cast dancers as those animals as they limped or lumbered about the floor.

By the twenties, the Charleston and the Lindy Hop had taken over, only to be replaced by Swing in the thirties and forties. Of course, polkas and waltzes never completely went away, remaining especially popular with immigrants.

In girls' summer camps, expressive dance was performed in the manner of the Modern Dance movement, beginning in the nineteenth century with Isadora Duncan and others. Girls danced for others, sometimes on a wooden floor, but often outside on the grass.

84]

This page: Two dancers, turn of the 20th century.

\* \* \*

Facing page photos, from top: Wequetong Club, often used for dancing; The Brooks, a dance club on Kid's Creek in Traverse City; O-At-Ka Beach on East Bay in Traverse City.

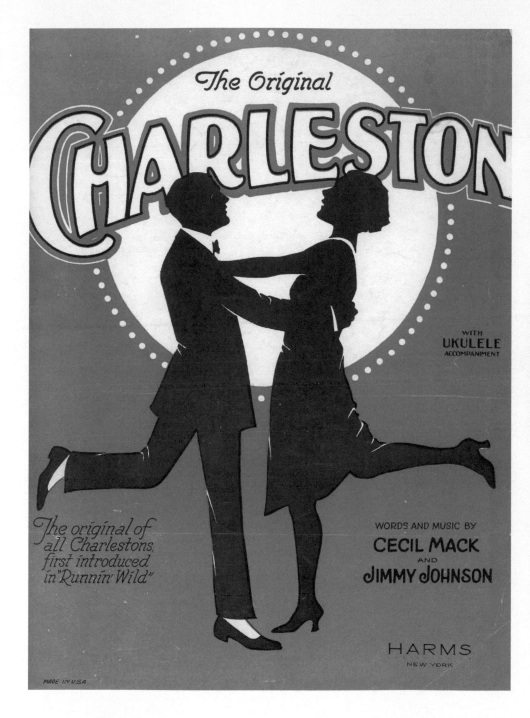

The Club House - Traverse City, Mich.

O-AT-KA BEACH, TRAVERSE CITY, MICH.

# GUILTY PLEASURES

## The FIRST PUFF

Proves to you that the *Stadium* is a mild cigar of **quality**.

Exaggeration has caused the failure of many advertised articles.

We do not claim for the Stadium that it is a 10 cent cigar for 5 cents. But we do claim that in buying it you get **full 5 cents worth**.

*Stadium* 5¢ Cigar

MUSSELMAN GROCER CO., DISTRIBUTORS.

## SOME CIGARS

are mild but lacking in.. quality. other cigars have quality but are..... strong. ▬ In the *Stadium* 5¢ Cigar

THIS IS THE EXACT SIZE AND SHAPE

mildness and quality have been combined

When you buy a....

*Stadium* 5¢ Cigar

You get full.... ..5 cents worth

*Stadium* 5¢ Cigar

MUSSELMAN GROCER CO., DISTRIBUTORS.

At the turn of the 20th century, cigars were far more popular than cigarettes even though cigarettes could be machine-made, while cigars were hand-rolled. The small town of Traverse City, Michigan, boasted nine cigar-manufacturing operations and one cigar box company at this time. Cigars connoted social power and influence; it was common for men to separate from the ladies after a dinner party to smoke cigars and discuss business or sports while the women to discuss more feminine pursuits — presumably matters pertaining to the household.

By the nineteen twenties, change was in the air. Cigarettes became associated with being modern, liberated, and sexy. Advertisements lured women to take up the habit. "Blow some my way!" a woman says to her man in a 1926 Chesterfield cigarette advertisement. The ad reportedly increased sales by 40 percent. In a short time, a cigarette became an accessory every bit as important as a string of beads or a feather boa.

Facing page: Al Barnes, Traverse City newspaper man, ca. 1950.
* * *
This page: Four gentlemen posing for the camera, three holding cigars, early 20th century.

Billiards and pool reached an early peak in popularity in the first two decades of the twentieth century. At this time, they were played by men, often young and unmarried. Immigrants from Eastern Europe enjoyed the game at a time of high immigration rates.

The games were associated with unsavory places like saloons. A Traverse City alderman contrasts the goodness of the public library with the evils of nearby temptations: "The original movement to establish a Carnegie library was largely in contemplation of providing a place in the central portion of the city where young people could spend their spare hours in pleasant surroundings and refining influences instead of lounging about the streets, pool rooms or saloons."

After declining in popularity during the thirties (when immigration slowed), the game came back in the latter half of the twentieth century as women and young people began to take it up.

Billiards game, ca 1900.

Americans consumed more alcohol in the first years of the New Republic than they do now — at least on a per capita basis. Fermented apple cider — hard cider — was a favorite drink of 19th century farmers. Historians believe distilled spirits were most popular at first, but beer soon overwhelmed all its competitors. Local breweries produced a variety of beers before brewing in Milwaukee and St. Louis came to dominate the business. Today, beer is still the most popular alcoholic beverage, outscoring wine in popularity 43 percent to 36.

The Volstead Act, passed in 1919, outlawed the production, transport, and sale of alcoholic beverages. During this time of Prohibition, numerous distilleries clandestinely continued to satisfy the drinking needs of the American people. "Bathtub gin" was just one of the many concoctions that were consumed by thirsty drinkers now separated from familiar bars and saloons. The Volstead Act was repealed in 1933.

Dunn's Bar, Traverse City, 1890.

WHO SAYS THAT THIS IS A DRY PLACE

Facing page: Grand Traverse sheriff and men with confiscated alcohol bottles.

* * *

This page: Humorous postcard.

# GRAND FESTIVAL OF FUN

## + Greatest Celebration Ever Known in Northern Michigan +

**JULY 4 1899**

**JULY 4 1899**

TRAVERSE CITY — WILL WELCOME YOU ALL

GRATEFUL FOR NATIONAL VICTORIES ON LAND AND SEA THE QUEEN CITY OF THE NORTH INVITES EVERYBODY TO CELEBRATE INDEPENDENCE DAY AT

# TRAVERSE CITY

## DARING BALLOON ASCENSION

This will be the most daring and thrilling event of the day. Miss Cleo Belmont, of the famous Belmont Sisters, will ascend in her balloon and while suspended in the air will perform the marvelous feat of Riding a Bicycle on a Trapeze Bar 2000 Feet Above the Earth. This wonderful and startling act is unparalleled in the history of mid-air exploits. It is a perilous and daring achievement.

## GAMES OF BALL

Morning and afternoon, between the GRAND RAPIDS DEMOCRATS, one of the strongest and best amateur teams in the state, and THE HUSTLERS, the favorites of Traverse City and Champions of Northern Michigan. These games will be played at the Twelfth Street grounds. An admission fee will be charged at both games.

## A GRAND PARADE

Will consist of Floats representing every phase of Commerce, Industry, Manufactures, Trades Unions, Military and G. A. R., Organized Civic and Fraternal Societies, Numerous Military and Martial Bands, Calithumpians and Horribles, and many other attractive and novel features. Prominent in the parade will be Battalions of Children carrying the National Colors. Children from the surrounding towns and country are cordially invited to join in this parade. To each one a Flag will be given which is to be kept and taken home.

## THE CALITHUMPIANS

Will make fun and noise. The noise and fun will begin at noon of the 3rd and continue until midnight of the 4th. Come early and stay late.

Details of the monster program and particulars of this great celebration can be had through the press notices and program announcements. Remember that the children are especially invited and are requested to join in the children's part of the parade, get a flag free to carry home and witness the day time Fireworks.

## DAY FIREWORKS AND HOT AIR BALLOONS

Immediately after the parade. This will be attractive to young and old. These Day Fireworks assume all manner of forms and shapes in mid-air. Human Figures, Animals, Dragons and many odd and grotesque figures. It will be a curious and interesting exhibition.

# Street Games, Bicycle Races, Aquatic Sports, with Prizes.

## Grand Military and Martial Bands Will Funish Music Throughout The Day.

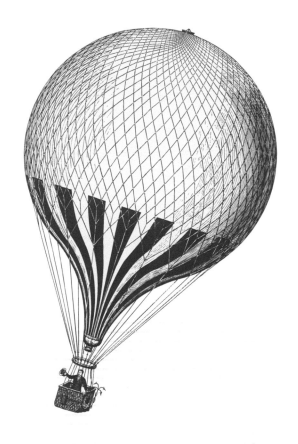

# CELEBRATIONS

Grand Traverse County fair, early 20th century.

At the turn of the twentieth century, entire towns turned out for the arrival of a railroad circus: schools let out, factories closed, businesses shut their doors. People would line Main Street to view the circus parade, a spectacle that featured elephants, camels, lions and tigers in cages, sword swallowers, tattooed men, strongmen, giants and dwarves, those who could spit fire, calliopes that caught the crowd up in "circus music," as well as a dozen clowns. Farmers would come in on wagons, bringing their whole families to view the show.

Circus elephants parade along Front Street in Traverse City, 1890's.

**TWELFTH STREET SHOW GROUNDS**

# Thursday, August 6th

# GENTRY BROS
## Famous Shows United

The circus brought a glimpse of the wider world to rural America, a glimpse distorted by the need to sell tickets to a public eager for spectacle and excitement. People saw tigers in cages, not in their native habitats. They saw blacks in the context of players in a circus band. They saw tableaus of Muslims in harems, Egyptians as pyramid dwellers, Santa Claus as a figure dressed in Russian costume, and Cinderella as she was portrayed in storybooks. In a time before radio and TV, the show reinforced stereotypes supplied in children's books and popular literature.

By the thirties, attendance at circuses had already begun to decline. Railroad circuses gave way to those brought by trucks, and the circus parade disappeared altogether. At any location shows were performed a few times at most, then packed away for the next town. Finally, unable to compete with spectacles brought by other media, the traveling circus largely disappeared in the United States. Its passing is mourned by those who experienced it.

Buffalo Bill's Wild West Show was another attraction that brought in enormous crowds. Skilled sharpshooters like Annie Oakley and Wild Bill Hickok showed off their talents as hundreds of citizens watched from the sidelines. Re-enactments of the Battle of Little Big Horn, featuring Chief Sitting Bull, captured the imaginations of young boys everywhere. The Wild West Show ended its tours in 1913, after a run that spanned 30 years.

Buffalo Bill's Wild West Show parade in Traverse City, 1898.

This page: William Frederick "Buffalo Bill" Cody, scout, bison hunter, and showman in Traverse City.

∗ ∗ ∗

Facing page: Annie Oakley, "Little Sure Shot of the Wild West" in Traverse City.

Marion Island, Traverse City, Mich.

No. 39  Publ. by Orson W. Peck, Traverse City, Mich.

Marion Island Pavilion (currently known as Power Island) was often visited by those celebrating the July Fourth holiday. Photo from the first decade of the 20th century.

The Fourth was celebrated with picnics and fireworks, much as it is today. In 1900 a parade was common in most towns, with Civil War veterans receiving the honors. Traverse City residents often took a boat ride to Marion Island in West Grand Traverse Bay to spend the evening dancing at a great pavilion. They would return home, exhausted on the last boat to depart, well after midnight.

Community picnics were held in the warm days of summer. Here are the headlines to a newspaper story about such an event conducted August 30, 1911, in Traverse City, Michigan.

GREAT CROWD AT PICNIC

TRAVERSE CITY DAY WAS HUGE SUCCESS

THOUSANDS HAD GOOD TIME
MEN, WOMEN AND CHILDREN
ENJOYED RECREATION

Stores and Factories Closed Most of Day

Greatest Gathering Ever on Grounds

Saw Thrilling Ball Game

BOARDMAN LAKE, TRAVERSE CITY, MICH.

Participants were invited to bring their own picnic goodies to the Civic Center (then called the Driving Park) for a day of fun. Farmers came with their families, and city folk, too. The rich and poor mingled. Young and old. Factory workers and their bosses. Estimates of the crowd varied between 8,000 and 10,000 people.

They ate and they partied. There were day fireworks and paper balloons launched for children, a bowery dance (a dance held outside) for the young, and the culminating baseball game for all who cared for that sport. There were no commercial or patriotic overtones to the celebration; it was simply an opportunity for people to get together.

Facing page: Picnic of employees of the Traverse City Hannah Lay company on Marion Island.

* * *

Above: Poplar Point, a popular picnic spot on Boardman Lake, about a half a mile south of the present Traverse City Public Library. Photo from the first decade of the 20th century.

A modest Christmas display, turn of the 20th century.

It is important to remember that workers put in 10 hour days in 1910, with few holidays observed throughout the year. Holidays were celebrated joyously, but not always with the same lavish expenditures as we do now. The Christmas tree tradition had been adopted by the twentieth century, though not all houses had them. Christmas presents did not form a mountain under the tree as they frequently do now, a few presents were exchanged among family members in a plain presentation.

A boy's Christmas, 1926. Photo courtesy Julie Schopieray.

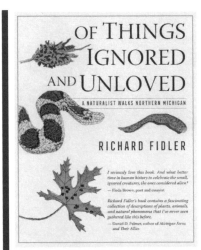

### OF THINGS IGNORED AND UNLOVED:
### A Naturalist Walks Northern Michigan

by Richard Fidler

This book will awaken the reader to events and things tuned out and forgotten in the noisy, rushing environment of our lives. It is a safari to nearby places.

"There are no insignificant beings, as Fidler so beautifully shows us." —Fleda Brown, poet and essayist

### HOW THIN THE VEIL:
### A Memoir of 45 Days
### in the Traverse City
### State Hospital

by Jack Kerkhoff
with an introduction by Ray Minervini

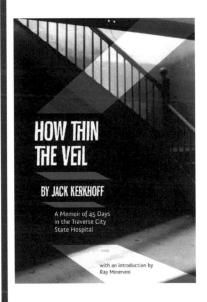

How Thin the Veil is a 45-day account of Kerkhoff's treatment, his conversations with the nurses and doctors (some of them with their real names), his interactions with the inmates, and his trips to downtown Traverse City watering holes. There's also romance in the form of Suzy, a pretty, lisping waif whose "bad spells" had kept her hospitalized for eight years.

First published in 1952, *How Thin the Veil* shines a hard-boiled light on the mid-century conditions of patients of mental illness.

### INSIDE UPNORTH:
### The Complete Tour, Sport and Country Living Guide to Traverse City, Traverse City Area and Leelanau County

by Heather Shaw, Jodee Taylor, Tom Carr

Our guide to all the things you need to know about Michigan's north country. This book was featured on Michigan Public Radio's "Stateside" program and chosen by Horizon Books' as a Michigan Notable Book in 2017. Find out where to eat, where to hike, where to shop and how to make maple syrup and find pretty rocks.

### BLOOD ON THE MITTEN:
### Infamous Michigan Murders, 1700s to Present
By Tom Carr

*In this hugely effective debut, Tom Carr sheds keen illumination upon a regional inventory of killers, kooks, cutthroats and the aggressively unhinged. The tales are horrific and humorous by turns — grisly, goofy, poignant dispatches expertly summated by a skilled veteran reporter who's no stranger to the back stairs habituated by a true sleuth. Story telling at its fully imagined best."* — Ben Hamper, bestselling author of *Rivethead*

# more books from mission point press

**POISON ON TAP:**
**How Government Failed Flint**
**and the Heroes Who Fought Back**

A Bridge Magazine Analysis of the Flint water crisis.

*Sometimes truth is stranger and scarier than fiction—such is the case with the Flint Water Crisis. Bridge Magazine staff painstakingly document one of the most significant cases of environmental injustice in U.S. history.*
*—Marc Edwards, Virginia Tech professor whose work helped prove that the regulators were wrong.*

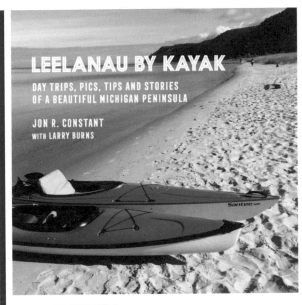

**LEELANAU BY KAYAK:**
**Day Trips, Pics, Tips and Stories**
**of a Beautiful Michigan Peninsula**

by Jon R. Constant
with Larry Burns

Beautiful photographs illustrate the lakeshore, Leelanau's many interior lakes and its three rivers.

Up to date directions and tips for all ages and expert

Maps and photos on every page.

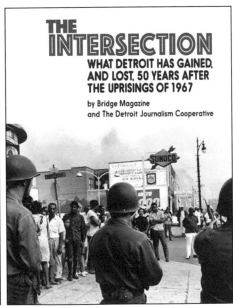

**THE INTERSECTION:**
**What Detroit has gained, and lost, 50 years after the uprisings of 1967**

By Bridge Magazine
and The Detroit Journalism Collective

*Fifty years after anger and frustration over police-community relations boiled over into a rebellion in Detroit, there are lots of people asking what we've learned, how we've changed.*

*This book, a collection of the coverage by the Detroit Journalism Cooperative during 2016, is a testament to that.* — From the Foreword by Pulitzer Prize-winning, Detroit native Stephen Henderson

**MISSION POINT PRESS BOOKS ARE AVAILABLE AT MICHIGAN BOOKSTORES AND AMAZON.**

CPSIA information can be obtained at www.ICGtesting.com
Printed in the USA
LVIW01n0939240918
591167LV00006B/11